This book is a Practical Step-by-Step Plan
to Build Inner Confidence
and Personal Power
to assist you to Live a Fantastic Life

CONTENTS

MERYDITH WILLOUGHBY

My primary goal when I became an independent consultant was to build an international business, develop my own business model, deliver services to executives globally and to write and contribute to the global media. Achieved.

I work with executives and Think Tanks globally and assist them to tackle issues that every executive and organisation faces. I am a change agent, and we work from the top down and from the bottom up. It is similar to what a chimney sweep does.

We ensure the mission statement is an active document and not just words typed and framed nicely.

We ensure that every level of employee has the same mindset, that they focus on collaboration, that they leave their ego at home, that they are authentic in their negotiations and in their conversations.

We ensure that they are contributing to the bigger picture and that they move forward together, to the next level while ensuring that the work they do is relevant, forward-thinking and conducive to improving the structure of the organisation, community and society in general. I have seen this in action, and it is stunning.

In addition to working with senior executives, I work with small groups and individuals. The process used is the same regardless of the number of people. It is a conversation style, and relevant topics are discussed for participants. Clients leave the session with their To Do list. Sessions are facilitated globally.

However, there is much more to me than this.

I discovered a raft of natural abilities while developing the above and was staggered to see the results that could be attained by clients when they worked hard and never, ever let doubts, insecurities or lack of knowing, get in their way.

I believe in the essence of human beings.

I know what is possible when you spend time supporting, loving, guiding an individual. No matter their age. No matter their background. No matter their societal status.

This is why I write books, spend many hours talking to people all around this wonderful world. This is why I have conversations on the radio and write many articles.

I want to pass my knowledge, experience, enthusiasm and passion onto you and everyone else on the planet. Together, we can make a difference. Together, we can assist ourselves and everyone else to develop their inner leader.

Do not let anyone dampen your enthusiasm and love for self, life, community and humanity.

Books

If it's to be: It's up to me
Back from Hell
Sex in the Boardroom
Thought Leadership

IF IT'S TO BE: IT'S UP TO ME

Knowing that most people are not taught how to develop a blueprint for their life or even how to live a life they would love in the 21st century is really quite shocking and the process woven through this book can help to change that. Society at all levels has to stop thinking (or not thinking) that people will just work it out and know what to do because it is clearly not working. If we applied the same fundamentals and include the emotional quotient that we apply to successful global corporations or bureaucracies who have learned to implement effective systems and processes and who regularly review and refine them and then always measure what they do qualitatively and quantitatively and link it to the bottom line, we would start the ball rolling in the right way. The key here is including the emotional bit, not deny it. Because without these life skills - life can be indeed a hell of a ride and the fantastic life I speak of often in *If it's to be: It's up to me*, is available to far too few.

1

LIVE YOUR FANTASTIC LIFE

You are *important,* you are *intelligent,* you are *wanted.* These are the three words that were repeated over and over to a little girl by her nanny while she was in her care, and then poignantly just before the nanny was to leave this little child's life forever. The nanny was the most important person in this child's life and was dismissed. The movie was in parts distressing because of the trauma the child was going through and the pain the nanny was experiencing. This movie was set in the 20th century. It touched my heart and you could see the desperation on the child's face when she and her nanny were having their final conversation and the earnestness with which the nanny delivered these three words again to the child – one final time – asking the child to repeat them after her. The last view we saw was of the little girl looking out of the window, face close to the pane of glass with tears streaming down her little cheeks, begging her nanny not to go, and with the nanny, heavy with heart and mind glancing back as she departed through the gate, one last time.

The little girl's heart was being torn apart because her nanny was leaving her and she was unable to comprehend the situation. She could do nothing to stop her. That decision had been made by her mother. All she knew was that someone she loved and adored had to go. The nanny knew that she had no power to change what was about to happen and did not know what was going to happen to the child when she was not there, but knew the power of self-belief and knew how incredibly important it was to remind the young child of the importance of these three words that she had repeated to the little girl often. Together they hurriedly repeated – you are *important*, you are *intelligent*, you are *wanted* – just before their lives were about to be irrevocably changed.

There are many people in society who have this level of pain to deal with. There are those who seem to have much less and there are those who seem to have a very fortunate life indeed. Regardless as to what your story is and which one it matches, the bottom line is that whatever you have experienced in your life – whether it is fantastic or not – you will have issues to address at every stage of your life, and the process detailed and discussed in *If it's to be: It's up to me*, can help you to do that.

You can learn how to fill yourself up to the brim and reprogram yourself second by second, minute by minute, day by day, month by month, year after year so that you learn how to live a life you love, that you learn how to develop your blueprint for your fantastic life, and that you teach yourself how to get through the other bits that are not as palatable.

You do not have to go through life believing that you cannot do it or be a victim of life. You can change if you are willing to do the work necessary to break through your road blocks and to keep pushing forward until you know what you want to do. Feel passion and enthusiasm running through your veins and keep moving forward, learn to expect success, tick off your successes, look back to observe and learn from the other days and experiences but do not allow them or other people's opinions, pre-conditioning, DNA, or road blocks get in your way. You develop your goals, your plans, keep yourself fit and healthy – do it and celebrate it and have the courage to do it your way and accept full responsibility for every thought and action you take.

But you know life can get in the way and life can throw us some curly issues that need to be dealt with. It can mean that we have to work very hard at relationships, work life stuff, making it all work, wider issues that need to be contended with, and health issues that can give us some challenges.

Throughout the fantastic times it is easy to be positive and remain calm; it is when the other times are being experienced that life can indeed go pear-shaped and things that we never dreamed of doing or experiencing are there to be dealt with.

It can be hard not to get caught up in being cynical about life and going down that route, and we can see our dreams and goals going up in smoke. However, if we arm ourselves with the skills and habits and behaviours that are necessary in order to combat issues and remain focused, alert, and proactive we have the best chance of truly being happy, living a life we love, having enough people in it who are important to us, and to living our fantastic life.

Knowing what you want is key to being able to live your fantastic life, and just as key is having the determination and never-give-up attitude. Without these (and you can learn them if they are not innate) you will be like far, far too many people who just give up because of a myriad of reasons they concoct in their mind.

Once you know what you want, you can then start planning, saving, and doing whatever it is that you need to do to execute your plan. Not knowing means that you could waste much of your precious time on this planet being busy, sitting on the fence, allowing fear to control you, allowing technology to dominate your life, allowing other things to get in the way, and allowing others to dictate what your fantastic life should look like.

You will see the word *think* written regularly throughout the book.

This is because thinking is an essential component to living any sort of quality life and certainly necessary if you are serious about changing yours.

It will underpin your success.

Thinking enables you to be deliberate and live your life with purpose.

Anyone I have spoken or listened to who has achieved a life that others envy tells the same story: they worked hard to achieve it. They went without much to do so. They were focused, passionate about what they did, and willing to do whatever it was that was required to achieve their goals. They never gave up, even when it was tough and took a long time to achieve their ultimate goal. They were not overnight successes. They will tell you that they continue to learn and fine-tune their systems and processes. They are always learning about themselves – good and other. They are regularly adapting to new circumstances.

One thing that has made a huge difference in my life for a very long time and certainly helps me to be successful and to stay on track is to look at people from all generations – observe how they behave, think, manage, and live their life, and if I don't like what I see and do not want to become like them, I make a mental note not to do whatever it is that I do not want to be like. It is important for me to be aware of what I want and do not want in my life, otherwise I am just playing follow the leader.

Other people can be a mentor for me.

This is a free, valuable resource.

I have noticed that, while I do not put my hand up for the tough bits of life, these periods are often the learning curves of my life and have taught me many things. They have taught me resilience and I am a much stronger and better person because of them. The key is to get through them in the first place and not to get stuck at any of the stages and believe that 'this is it'.

I do not wish to stay in the difficult periods any longer than I need to and have somehow got out of the ones I wanted to work on even when the issues seemed insurmountable.

I made a decision that I would not allow that feeling of being frozen by fear control me and to stop me from doing what is important to me. I committed to myself that I would do what I need to do to push through it if the issue is important enough and part of my fantastic life plan, regardless of how challenging it is.

I became aware of the benefit of using a pragmatic approach with everything I do years ago, and am committed to a systems and processes approach in every area of my life. I know now what can be waiting on the other side and to me there is nothing more important than unravelling my authentic self and being determined to be true to what I believe is right.

Think of the work you do with this book as a beginning point, not an end point; give your attitude a thorough spring clean regularly, teach yourself how to adapt to what is happening around you, and have a fantastic time while you are working on your personal development model – your blueprint. The process can be used at any stage of your life.

Once you have learned and understand the process, you can change it to suit your own style and then continue to adapt it to suit your purpose.

If it's to be: It's up to me, was developed as a result of working with many people all over the world over many years and at many levels of society. Having done so, I found that there are a number of processes you can use in your life that can make the difference between living a fantastic life and a ho-hum one. While we are on this planet we may as well be working on our goals and doing what we feel passionate about.

Throughout this book, I will discuss key concepts that people act upon when they live a life they love, and I will give you tools and ideas you can use. Let's have fun together while you are learning how to put the process into place.

What I need from you is a commitment that you will work hard, be honest with yourself, challenge yourself,

and do whatever else it takes to achieve your fantastic life. You will need to tweak certain aspects of it until it is right, and you will also need to know that to live a fantastic life takes a huge amount of courage, commitment, dedication, determination, passion, enthusiasm, time, and energy.

If you have these attitudes and qualities or are willing to develop them, then you are likely to do very well when you work with the process woven throughout the book.

If you want to live a fantastic life but are not willing to put the hard work in, then you are likely to achieve little or no change and be disappointed with the results you get.

In some chapters you will be given questions to consider, in others I will provide case studies, and analogies will be woven throughout the book.

The initial phase of the project is over a 10-week period. This will give you enough time to work on two *small* goals and get used to the process. It is important that you realise that this is only the commencement and much learning will continue as you strive to become expert over your own life, while developing your own personal development model

– your blueprint – and continuing to refine and define it as you need to adjust to changing circumstances and as you become more aware of what you want with an ever increasing number of insights and 'ah hah' moments.

It is *very important* that you do not jump into action before you have completed reading the book and studied the questions at least twice. Getting into action without thorough preparation is why people do not succeed with their goals and why the 'New Year's Resolutions' statistics are as they are. The planning and thinking part of the goal is far more important initially than the action component.

The 10-week period is only a taste of what your life can be like and what you can achieve if you are willing to work very hard, make yourself a priority, be committed to doing this each and every day for the rest of your life, and do what is important to you.

You may wonder what you are doing when you start, and that is normal; it is like anything: the more you do, the better you will get at it. When you can see how far you have come, you can look back and say 'wow, I did that'.

I look forward to assisting you to start thinking about what it is that you need to do to be able to live a life you love, and where, over time, you can become confident enough to develop your own personal development model – your blueprint, your fantastic life – that works for you and which you revisit regularly and fine-tune as required. That is always my goal for anyone I work with: to assist them to develop their own model rather than follow in someone else's footsteps.

2

GETTING STARTED

ave you noticed that often successful people are positive, inspiring, clear about what they want to achieve, and go from one successful venture to the next? They seem to have a confidence that radiates from them and are generous with their knowledge and experience. They continue to keep doing what they love and to achieve their dreams and goals. They seem not to understand the concept of 'can't', or cannot be deterred by failures. But guess what: that's their outward appearance. When you scratch the surface, they all have insecurities and a lack of confidence at times and the same stuff that the rest of us have to deal with.

They are not immune from it. They have simply learned the recipe for their success.

After observing and working with many successful people, I have also noticed that there are other similarities. They don't wait for someone else to tell them to get started and they don't expect someone else to do it for them. They get the right people on their team and they just do it. They are willing to keep going when things get tough, when they get bored, when changes aren't happening fast enough, and they are also willing to keep trying until they are successful.

They don't whinge and moan; they just get on with it.

Certainly, there will be many things that impact us as we live our life, but you know what nevertheless each day requires: that we get up in the morning and that we go to bed at night, with a certain number of hours to fill in between dawn and dusk.

And we will do it all again and again. It is largely a decision that we make each day, and it is largely dependent on our attitude and belief in ourselves.

In this chapter, *Getting started*, think about when you did something in your life that made you feel fulfilled, where you just loved it and enjoyed the moment. It might have been spending time with someone you care about, going for a holiday, preparing a lovely meal, or being employed in a job that you love.

Start thinking about a life you have only ever dreamt about – your fantastic life. And start dreaming, start getting excited about how you are going to fill in the time between getting up and going to bed.

Start small. Get used to success. Start to expect it. Start to love it. And start to do more of the things that will bring it to you.

But mainly, commit to yourself that you will do whatever it takes, that you will be patient with yourself, and that you will start to treat yourself like you treat your best friend.

You can use the process in *If it's to be: It's up to me*, over and over again throughout every stage of your life to achieve your dreams and goals – whether it is for your professional or personal life.

I will help you. I will support you. I will guide you.

You may feel challenged at times, but always remember that no one else can do it for you. You are the only person who can make it happen.

This is the beginning of the rest of your life.

Purchase a specific workbook and have separate sections for each chapter. Use the workbook only for this work.

It can be a valuable reference point for you now and for the rest of your life. You will be able to benchmark memories and reflect on just how far you have come since you started, and by reading it regularly you will gain insights about yourself and about other changes you would like to make. I find this an incredibly powerful tool and have used this method for years now. I love going back and reading where I was years ago and noting the changes that I have made. Life goes by so quickly and it is easy to forget all about advances we have made because what we are doing now soon becomes our new normal. It is far too easy to focus only on the changes that we want to make.

I am so glad I spent the time working out the above because it has held me in good stead for years now and certainly gives me hope and confidence when I am going through a tough period or day. Writing down my thoughts and being concise with what I want has also made a huge difference.

Being clear about what we want is what it is all about. It saves years of head-banging experiences and wasting years or decades thinking about what we want to do rather than just doing it.

We all make mistakes – that is normal. They are integral to our success. We need to learn from them and the more we take on, the more we will make. That's just the way it goes. Learning from them helps us to mature and to develop wisdom and to be even clearer about what we want and need to do.

People who don't try anything probably won't make mistakes because they don't put themselves out there. But think about the life they'd lead. Is that for you?

I could not imagine anything worse. I would die of boredom.

Because of our experience at school and in our early days, we swallow the myth that 'if we make a mistake we're stupid', and sadly I see far too many people at all stages of their life coming from this perspective.

We are not stupid if we make a mistake.

Don't allow other people to make you feel this way. Know that you are stepping out of your comfort zone and, of course, you will make mistakes.

But who cares?

They are all just learning lessons, and the more self-confidence and self-esteem we develop – while the mistakes can still sting – we can teach ourselves to care less about what others think and about the mistakes we make.

We learn over and over again that we can continue to pick ourselves up and get on with it.

When I am at the beginning point of a new goal – when I am getting started – it can be a difficult time if I don't have a clue what I need to do or how I will achieve it. It is frustrating; I can feel cranky, and my self-esteem and confidence may not be as high as I want. My mind can give me constant negative thoughts and I can hear the naysayer's words clearly. At that point I have a choice: I can stay there, or I can push through. No doubt you will know what my choice is if I have decided that this goal is something I want.

I now know that the above is only because I don't know what I'm doing. It stirs up things in my unconscious mind that I have no idea about and, when I'm working on achieving the goal, this initial part of the process can feel like pulling teeth.

I can feel as though I am never going to know what to do, because the path ahead is so foggy. When I stick with it, all of a sudden I gain some clarity and then things seem to make more sense. I am then delighted that I stayed with the process.

So, let's go – let's get started.

IF IT'S TO BE: IT'S UP TO ME

Set a time to start.

Put a time in your diary for a personal weekly meeting for one hour each week for the next 10 weeks where you will be undisturbed – mobile off – where you feel relaxed, and where you allow yourself to get excited about the possibilities.

This is the most important meeting you will have, so make it that way in your mind. Prepare for it and go out somewhere that will reflect the important occasion. Somewhere out of your normal environment.

This changes how you feel and stops you from doing little things that just take your attention away from what you're working on. It also gives you an opportunity to think about things while you are on your way to it, and then again when you return to your other responsibilities.

It's your time so make the most of it.

And don't let anything stop you from starting.

Write down what your professional and personal life comprises of at the moment. Be specific: no drama – just what's happening.

For example: relationships at work and out of work, career, fitness, health, stress levels, confidence, travelling, hobbies, work life, social activities, finances, health, creativity.

It's not good or bad – it just is. Write it down so that you can see what's happening in your whole life at the moment.

After careful consideration, choose two specific areas and think, long and hard, about what you would like to be different in these areas and what can be achieved in the next 10 weeks.

Write this down in one sentence for each area, noting what you'll have when you achieve it.

For example: 'making myself a priority and loving it.' 'An office so tidy I know where everything is.'

Remember to start with two goals that are small so that you will be successful. Do a lot of dreaming without guilt, without question, just because you can and see what comes into your mind.

What are two things that you can work on in a 10-week period that will make you feel proud of yourself when you have achieved them?

What you are doing now is getting used to the process in *If it's to be: It's up to me,* and starting to embed it into your unconscious mind and, over time and with much practise, it can assist you to achieve your goals – any size and in any area of your life.

You are starting to teach yourself to expect success, to be successful, and, most importantly, to plan for it.

A key to living your fantastic life is to spend time working out what it is that you want and reflect regularly. What it will look like, what it will feel like, what it will taste like (metaphorically speaking, of course), and then, bit by bit – tiny bits sometimes, other times big chunks – create it.

Most people have too many big goals and never achieve them, thus they feel like failures. Start with small goals and build up to big and enjoy the process.

The criteria for each goal need to be something that you would love, something that will make a difference to your life.

It might be something that you have wanted to do for a long time, but you haven't known how to start and are not sure how to do it.

It also needs to be measurable, inspiring, realistic, and something that you will hold yourself accountable to.

It always takes more than the first week for clients to become clear about what they are doing, what they need to do, and the strategies to get them there.

It's often not until week four or longer that the penny really drops. And until the penny does drop, you just keep moving forward.

Here are some questions to help you with the process.

- What are the goals you have chosen?
- Do they meet the criteria of a goal - inspiring, realistic, achievable, and measurable?
- What will you have when you've got them?
- What will be different in your life?
- How will you know when you've achieved them?
- How will you feel when you've achieved them?
- How will you feel if you don't stay with the process?

In the last 10 minutes of your personal weekly meeting, develop an action plan or a To Do list for yourself that identifies what you need to do in the next week that will take you closer to achieving your goals.

Keep it brief and concise so that you don't feel as though you're overloading yourself.

On this action plan, identify:

- Who are the key people you need to contact to get your goals to the next level?
- What specific things do you need to do?
- Put a date next to each action as to when you will have completed it.
- Look at your plan every day.
- Keep it close-by and tick things off as you complete them.

Many clients say that this is key to their success because it is something that is tangible and they can see whether they've done it or not.

Lists get the emotion out of it – you've either done it or you haven't. They are powerful because they stop the thoughts racing around in your head and they start to assist you to gain clarity in your life.

You also learn to prioritise things and learn what is important, what isn't important, what could be done, and what doesn't need to be done at all.

Excellent: you've started and you've had one meeting with yourself – well done.

Now, let's prepare for your second personal weekly meeting.

Read the previous information of this chapter and get out your workbook, noting:

- What have you actually achieved in the past week that will get you closer to your goals?
- Were you able to do everything on your action plan?
- If you were, what were the outcomes?
- If you weren't, why not?
- Did you put too many things on it in the first place?
- Give yourself a tick when you've done what you said you'd do. Doing this makes you feel good and it's such a powerful feeling when you do what you said

you'd do. I even put a smiley face on it because it does just that – puts a smile on my face.

- What have you learned about yourself, good – other?

If you didn't do some of the actions, think about what prevented you – be accountable to yourself and go through why you didn't. Be honest with yourself.

It may be that you decided that the action wasn't necessary and that's okay, so just put 'no' next to it. That can be just as powerful as the tick because you've made a decision not to do something that would not get you closer to your goals.

If, however you didn't do them because you didn't make them a priority, then think about the price that you're paying and decide whether you want to continue not doing what you believe to be essential to your success.

This isn't about giving yourself a hard time or getting caught up in guilt, it is just to get to know yourself better and to be accountable to yourself.

This is where you start to give yourself positive feedback just like you would if your friend, colleague, or child had done something that you were proud of. You do this even for very small successes because it starts to build your confidence and self-esteem and you start to get used to treating yourself with respect and kindness.

Focus on what you have done – not what you haven't done. This starts to build a half glass full approach to life and is worth every second of investment.

As an ongoing strategy, note how you're feeling as you progress through the weeks – what's changing, what you know now that you didn't know when you first started using the process in the book.

For example:

- Are you starting to feel a little more confident that you will achieve your goals?
- Are you letting people know what you want?
- Are you letting people know what you expect from them?
- Are people commenting about changes they have noticed in you?
- Are you starting to make yourself a priority?

- Can you see that you are slowly-but-surely changing any of your thought processes?

It is essential that you make yourself a priority regardless of what else is happening in your life. There will always be competing priorities and something that should be done and if you don't make yourself a priority, you'll continue to get what you've always got and that's not why you purchased *If it's to be: It's up to me*, in the first place.

If you are not giving yourself at least 30 minutes each day to spend thinking about your life, ask yourself: why not?

Follow the same process each week for 10 weeks and pace yourself, noting what you've done and what you have to do so that you will achieve your goals in this period.

Initially, you may find it difficult and wonder what you're doing but when you stay with the process – from what my clients say and from my own experience – clarity is gained because you learn what to do and you learn what does and what doesn't work for you.

Why not think of yourself as an Olympic athlete? Focus on what you want to achieve, plan for it to happen, set that plan into action, notice what's happening and what you're doing to achieve your goals and be absolutely single minded that you are going to succeed. In a sense, you're in a better position than an Olympic athlete because they work for years to win, not knowing whether they'll ever end up being successful, because in their sport, there's only one winner.

Use the process in *If it's to be: It's up to me*, over and over again and all throughout your life. Share your skills with everyone you know. Teach your kids these skills from the moment they are born.

HABITS

As I have continued to unravel the human condition and learned more about human behaviour, habits, and what is possible, I have found that there is never a shortage of new data being published. I have read much and learned much and, as more information becomes available, it is mind-blowing to think that much of what we have been taught is simply not true. One such article I found detailing how complex the human brain is and the process used, second to second, astounded me. It turns much previous learning on its head. When we understand what is possible, when we challenge the status quo, when we are willing to put the hard work in, when we don't do as we are told just because someone tells us that it is right for us, we do not have to be passive passengers – we can be the driver of our life and experience as a human being. We can be the driver of our mind and brain. The brain is malleable. We are capable of much more than we think we are and certainly much more than what we have been taught. When we continue to learn and respect our forebears for what they already knew and couple that with 21st technology and knowledge, we are in for an exciting time that will revolutionise society as we know it now.

The brain is the most complex organ in the human body. It produces our every thought, action, memory, feeling and experience of the world. This jelly-like mass of tissue, weighing in at around 1.4 kilograms, contains a staggering one hundred billion nerve cells, or neurons. The complexity of the connectivity between these cells is mind boggling. Each neuron can make contact with thousands or even tens of thousands of others, via tiny structures called synapses. Our brains form a million new connections for every second of our lives. The pattern and strength of the connections is constantly changing and no two brains are alike. It is in these changing connections that memories are stored, habits learned and personalities shaped, by reinforcing certain patterns of brain activity, and losing others. (Phillips, 2006)[1]

Think of a new habit as making a new connection in your brain. Initially that new connection will not be strong and it will take much practise to cement it into your unconscious mind. Think about a baby who is learning to hold a spoon and the mess they make in learning that new skill. How many times do they practise before they get it right, how much mess do they make, how many bibs need changing,

---

1   Phillips, 2006, viewed 15 May 2008, <https://www.newscientist.com/article/dn9969-introduction-the-human-brain>.

how much encouragement do we as carers give them, and how much excitement do we exhibit when a well-practised skill has been mastered?

That is the same when we are forming new habits and going through the motion of learning how to do something we need to do in order to achieve our goals (consciously or not), or consciously changing the ways that we want to behave and therefore create a new habit more suitable to us now. It can take us a long time before the changed or new habit is entrenched and before we feel competent and confident with it. And, as with the baby, we need to give ourselves just as much support and encouragement as our carers first did with us when we were learning all of those now incredibly basic habits and behaviours but which have given us the foundation for our life, and which were conditioning us from our parents' model and view of life.

There is no doubt that many people do want to change habits and behaviours and look for many ways to do this. And no doubt there is no shortage of personal development information distributed. While indeed there are many well-researched personal development books, programs, and workshops on the market, there are also many that do not tell the honest story about living a fantastic life. Many are full of spin. This advertising material and books may be seductive but they give people false hope.

I regularly hear and read that it only takes a few weeks to change a habit – that it is easy – and I regularly read articles or see advertising in the media that say in 12 weeks or less you can change your bad habits and behaviours and a new life will miraculously appear.

This is particularly common around the beginning of the New Year.

Reading this sort of information is concerning on many levels. There is no explanation as to what a habit is or guidance to assist you go to go deeper and understand why you are doing what you are doing in the first place. It is a magic formula, like the shake-and-mix drink that promises to help you lose 30 kilos in a short period of time. It is said that over 90% of people regain that weight lost and more in 12 months because they did not change the underlying issue that was causing the weight gain in the first place – the habits and behaviours and attitudes behind it.

Without understanding why you have the habits in the first place, taking responsibility for them, and working to change what you do not want, it is unlikely that the magic formula will do much other than be a feel-good-factor in the short term and a possible deterrent for what you really could achieve in the long term if you set your mind to it and really focused on the issues you want to address.

I have never found a habit that has completely disappeared and not returned under the right conditions.

We live in such a fast-paced society where things happen quickly and where technology is on steroids and the quick fix advertising fits in nicely. Many people want to believe the magic formula, and then what happens if it is not successful? What happens if under different conditions the habit comes back? What does that do to the person's confidence and self-esteem?

If it is said often enough, if it is passed down from generation to generation, if we see it advertised enough, why wouldn't we believe it? That is how the marketing and advertising machine works and works brilliantly.

Do not be fooled by such trickery.

We are not educated as to what reaction we may receive from other people because we have changed. We are pigeonholed by all of whom we associate with. I do it, no doubt you do it. That is the way it is with human beings. Within a few seconds, we have slotted anyone we meet into their pigeonhole and we may or may not be right, but once we have done that it is hard to change what we believe to be true. If we have known the person for a long time and, suddenly, they embark on a change program, then it can be very hard for people to get used to the new you and it will take time for everyone to adjust. That is, if they ever do.

There is no short cut to living your fantastic life.

If you want change in your life and want to live a fantastic life and maintain it, then it will take you much time and energy and it will always be a work in progress. When you realise that you have to put as much time into your personal development as you do your professional life, caring for your family, looking after your home, keeping yourself fed, exercised and cared for in all of the other ways necessary, you are on the right track.

I know that as a human being I am made up of more habits
than I could count – or possibly ever hope to know what
my unconscious mind and body have stored – and if I
want to change the ones I am aware of, I need to become
conscious of what I want to change it to, and be willing to
go through the stress and anxiety of it and to stay with
the process at each point of changing the habit to a more
functional one. While it may be a little easier for me now
because I have been doing it for a long time, it is never easy
and I have to always be vigilant with those habits that have
not served me well.

They are patient and lie in wake in the background, ready to
become active immediately if I fall by the way.

I know that, when I become conscious of a habit and all of
the associated behaviours that go along with habits and
am absolutely determined to stop doing whatever it is,
it can feel like I am teasing a tightly-knitted scan of wool
apart: it is confusing and disorientating, and when I am
going through this process, I feel stressed and anxious
about it, with little clarity until I get to a few stages down
the track. I wonder what I am doing. I do not feel confident
at this point because I do not have clarity. I need to spend a

significant amount of time thinking about it and reflecting on what I am trying to do and at each stage along the way.

In addition to this, when I check in with my thoughts and become aware that I am about to embark on a venture I do not want (unwanted awakened behaviour), I need to think about it first – not react or respond to the person or situation – and make a conscious decision as to what I need and will do. It is important to be clear in my mind as to what would and could happen if I take one step forward.

When I do this, I feel proud of myself and take a huge sigh of relief because I know what I have just stopped myself from having to go through. It is a victory and all of these little victories add up to me living my life the way I want and give me freedom to be all of who I am rather than bogged down with other people's stuff and then having to extricate myself after having become immersed in the quagmire yet again.

I need to continue to pay full attention and to stop allowing other people or society to dominate how I think or do what I think they expect of me and stand up for what I truly believe in and put the hard work into changing what I do not want. Strong personal boundaries are essential when you are committed to changing habits, because there always seems to be someone who will test you out, to see whether you mean what you say.

Often over the years, when I have teased apart habits and behaviours I want to change or review, I have become aware that they seem to be upside down and nothing like I would have expected. One example of this, as I continued to unravel unwanted habits, is that I became aware that when someone treated me badly – or if they were abusive (verbally) – I would feel responsible for what had happened, take ownership of the problem, and then set about fixing it. I remember that guilt was a big part of this as well.

I do not deliberately practise this behaviour and, while I would love to be able to tell you that it is never an issue, I cannot. I need to pay full attention to this habit and its associated behaviours and, if I know that a situation could generate an outcome I do not want and could lead me back into the wilderness, I take charge of the situation and manage it accordingly.

As I unravelled this habit it was interesting, because when I had become aware of it not only did I realise that my thought process was upside down, there was also quite a bit of shame about it, because I thought I was the only one who behaved in this manner. However, when I moved through it, I noticed many people behaved in this manner and were not aware of what they were doing.

Why would I now notice this behaviour when I didn't before? It is because before it was normal for me, hence I didn't see it. And now that it is not normal for me, I notice other people playing out that role often and think how glad I am that I do not do it.

When I have broken through a habit it can seem so clear and I think to myself: how easy was that and why did I do that for so long? However, that is the mind's (or other people's) way of minimising what I have done – the hard work and the tenacity it took to break through. I am not fooled by that thought at all now.

The barriers and road blocks can feel huge at times when breaking through a habit. When you are working on it, you can think that it will never happen because it can be such hard work and because that habit and behaviour is so much a part of you. But when you have made it to the other side, it is indeed wonderful and many other terrific things can follow.

The reason I continue moving forward and doing what I say in this book is because I have tasted success and happiness, and each time I break down a habit and associated behaviours, remain vigilant, I taste more of it. I know what it is like to feel the magic of life and I want as much as I can have of this for all of my life and at each stage of it.

Daily Habit Tracker

The hard work, the tenacity required, the uncertainty is the same whichever side of the fence you sit on, and I know which side of the fence I will stay on and work towards. I know that sitting on the fence is even worse than being on either side of it because when you do not make a decision either way, you can be locked into inaction and maybe never free of what the issue is.

I know that however conscious I think I am, however much personal and professional development I do and have done, that, really, I have no idea as to everything that is in my unconscious mind, or how I have been conditioned by all and sundry. I work hard, do the best I can and look at the results I have in my life. If I do not like the results I am getting in my life, I can change if it is important to me, and if not: so be it. Learning does not stop when we leave school. It continues throughout every part of our life whether we are aware of it or not. We can harness it and live with passion and purpose each and every day of our life. We can fuel our love of knowledge and continue to learn and expand our horizon each and every day of our life.

If it is said often enough, if it is passed down from generation to generation, if we see it advertised enough, why wouldn't we believe it? That is how the marketing and advertising machine works and works brilliantly. Do not be fooled by such trickery.

4

STAYING FOCUSED

t is not surprising that people have so much trouble staying focused in the 21st century. There are so many things vying for our attention and so many things that you can become involved with and addicted to. If you are a driven person with many interests, it will be even harder for you. It is enough to make you feel ill even if you only try to keep up with a tiny percentage of what is happening in the world. The information comes at us from every direction and at a manic pace; add the way that technology is advancing and what is now available and what will become available in the next decade, it is now more important than ever to remain vigilant and extremely focused. Not to do so means that you are likely to become a New Year's Resolution statistic.

I am no different from you and what I find is that I have to be constantly aware of what is trying to take my attention away from my plans and goals. I need to be still, think, unwind, and relax otherwise I get caught up in it without even being conscious of it. I now know that I have to have regular time off each week. During that time off I invariably have insights and become aware of how I was getting caught up in stuff that will not help me to achieve my goals. I can then make the changes necessary and am back; I am focused again.

When I started my business, I had to make some tough decisions. I am the sort of person who masters something and then likes to move on. Professionally, I do that in general by the end of 12 months and am then looking to do something else. However, I knew that I could not do that if I was to be taken seriously in the area I chose to work in and to become skilled at it. Some of the questions I pondered regularly were: how could I stay with what I love and not get bored? How could I continue to feel the passion and enthusiasm running through my veins that gives me the energy to do what I want and need to? How could I manage the tedious bits, and discipline myself to work the hours necessary to build my business to the level I wanted?

What I decided I could do that would give me the above was to keep learning and educating myself in topics under the umbrella of leadership development. Initially, I decided that I would complete some study which would link to what I had already done – formal and informal.

While I have always felt passionate about learning and have done so in many areas, it was not until I was a mature age student that I went to gain an undergraduate degree. It was an incredible experience and changed my life. After enrolling and just before I commenced studying, I was given some sage advice; I was told not to go in the front door and out the back, which meant get actively involved in many other areas on campus rather than just going for the sole purpose of gaining a degree. I followed this sage advice. My five years at the university was an incredible, wonderful, life changing experience, and I would not be where I am today professionally or personally without it.

When I had completed the degree, and then later when I was wearing the academic gown and holding my parchment, it was a magical moment shared with family, other students, and friends.

Because I started formal study at the midpoint in my life, it was challenging to do along with everything else. When I reflect on this period of my life and see it in my mind's eye, the view that comes to me is a road – a long straight road – with a small round microscopic element on the side that represented what I was doing for myself. The rest of my time and life was committed to other people and other areas. Everything at university did place an extra burden on me and I do remember that my stress levels were far too high, however that time was for me and intuitively I knew that it was right.

I did achieve many things through this period and it was fantastic. I met many people I would never have otherwise met, had a range of experiences I would never have otherwise had, stretched myself to the limit, and had much fun.

Without the support of the academics, I would not have been able to complete this degree. I was unable to source all of the childcare that I required because of the subjects I took in the evening and often I had to take my young children with me. The academic who lectured in these subjects went out of his way for us and provided the kids with videos to watch.

In addition to this, as I have moved out of the parenting role, it is clear that this degree set me up for success in every other stage of my life because of the learnings that took place and the things I have done since that period.

Because I stuck with it, I am an incredibly different woman. It is rewarding to think just how many other people's lives have been changed because of it. It impacts every single person I ever come in contact with or work with because of the knowledge, education, and skills attained.

Since this time, I have fuelled my love of learning and gained a cross-institutional postgraduate qualification in education and politics from three major universities. Other studies are many and varied. My informal interests and education continues on a daily basis and links into everything else I have done.

Living this way underpins what I do each and every day and I feel privileged to be able to work with people at all levels of society and in a range of capacities. It is always rewarding for me to be able to clearly show clients how being focused can determine the quality of the life they can live and the goals they can achieve throughout every stage.

I continue to be astounded at what is possible with human beings when they are given the support, love, guidance, and encouragement they need in order to gain focus, giving them the ability to build, develop, and maintain a blueprint for their life.

When I managed a youth mentoring project, I saw lives turn around because of the guidance and love they received from their mentor, who helped the kids to focus on their school work and think about other areas of their life. It was my role to source mentors for students in six schools, plus the principal project school. Over a period of two years, I secured 100 mentors from all walks of life. I trained and developed the mentors and they, in turn, worked with their students. Most mentors stayed with their student for up to a year – one mentor stayed with her student for five years – and the changes were phenomenal.

At the other end of the spectrum, I saw an 88-year-old woman become so inspired by her life once again that she was overwhelmed by the projects we did together. I loved spending time with her. She loved me reading the chapters of my books and other articles I had written to her, and I loved reading to her. We had so much in common and to talk about. I learned much from her, enjoyed her company, and could have listened to her for hours. I loved our deep and meaningful conversations. There appeared to me to be no age difference or barrier, and at times we acted like kids and laughed our heads off. As each project came to an end, she started new ones, and 12 months after we commenced spending time together, she continued to work on what she loved and did not require assistance from me.

It gave her many new things to talk about with her loving, supportive family, and they were delighted to see her this happy and fulfilled. This lovely woman said that the process I used helped her to learn how to live her life, and her saying that confirmed to me that it doesn't matter how old or young you are, there will always be issues that need to be addressed, and that we all need help to focus on what is important to us.

In my corporate role, I work with senior executives, and the results are just as effective when they learn the basics of living and breathing and being committed to a systems and processes approach, and linking everything they do to the business bottom line. They learn that this approach is just as important in their personal life, and are often blown away by what they can achieve when they use this approach every day.

As a young woman, I decided that I wanted to change behaviours and habits and started on a personal development quest. Years later I found out that the model I had taught myself was a process and called CBT. It is powerful and one worth investigating. Through this, I have taught myself how to stay focused, to re-frame my thoughts, and become aware if I have put negative connotations or excess emotions onto something. I have found that I have to pay attention to my thoughts but not get bogged down in them. I have to remember that they are just thoughts, and, without intervention, have no control over me. If I am being negative about something I can then turn that thought into a positive statement. While I cannot control the thoughts in my head – they can drive me nuts at times – I am in total control as to what comes out of my mouth and I practise the *Zip it* model which I developed and discuss in *Sex in the Boardroom*.

This process has also taught me to re-examine many things that have occurred in my life and to become aware that, while I cannot change history, I can change my reaction to it. It is clear that the brain does not always file things accurately, and as an adult I have re-examined many of these and notice that they were filed from a child, adolescent perspective, and by re-examining them I have been able to file them from an adult perspective. Doing this has made a huge difference to me and I have been able to re-frame memories and experiences which have added to the quality of my life.

While living this way may seem time consuming – and it certainly is – after observing people who do not use this process, because either they haven't been taught or think it is not relevant for them, I would not choose to live any other way. To do so would ensure that I just get caught up in the stuff of life.

The time to start planning your life is all the time. Not when you are over certain aspects of it and then want the next bit to roll out immediately and not be willing to put the required effort into it. Or be so stressed that you are not aware of what you are doing or even know that you are like this because adrenalin has taken over. If you are feeling like this at any time, the question to ask yourself is: why you have let it get to this point in the first place? Always take your actions back to square one and take full responsibility for what is happening. It is not conducive to living your fantastic life when you rush into goal setting and development and expect it to just happen, not put the amount of time or research required into it. Living like this may see you missing out on many opportunities you would love, and settle instead for second best because you didn't put the appropriate time or strategies in place, and that is not what staying focused is all about.

WHAT CAN YOU DO TODAY TO BRING YOU ONE STEP CLOSER TO YOUR GOAL

The busier we are, the less likely we are to spend time thinking.

It is not valued in our current society and often considered a waste of time. When you are sitting and thinking in the workplace you are likely to be thought of lazy and inept and your job could be jeopardised, and so of course you transfer this thought process to your personal life. In our personal life, once we've moved through the child and adolescent stage, it is unlikely that we will be encouraged to spend time thinking deeply about our life and what's happening in the world around us and what we really want to be doing and achieving in and with our life.

We may even be thought to be odd if we do spend hours thinking.

I love thinking, and spend hours doing it because it underpins my life.

It is the catalyst for me to work out what's really happening, what's important, and to put everything into perspective. It is never a waste of my time. It helps me to stay focused and is key to me living my fantastic life. To not do so is wasting my life and that is something I will not do.

Being focused is key to living your fantastic life. It has little to do with luck. It is staying with the process until you are clear about what it is that you want to do, but not getting stuck in 'not being clear'. While you are in that mode, keep moving forward anyway and keep researching until you have the insights you need. Clarity comes with practise, determination, and discipline. It is being realistic and respecting yourself enough that you make yourself a priority. It is okay to do that. Put as much effort into you as you always have with everyone else. It is important that you do that. Think personal development model all of the time. Think personal weekly meeting every week. Do what you love. Live your life with passion and purpose.

EXPECT SUCCESS

f we do not consciously expect success and implement strategies to create it then, in one way or another, we may well be unconsciously sabotaging ourselves. We may well allow other people to dominate our life and determine our future. That is not what this book is about. *If it's to be: It's up to me*, is intended to assist you to unravel who you are and to stand tall and be proud of who you are – just as you are right now – and as you continue to change as you implement any changes you deem necessary. Not changes that others have said are necessary, but changes that *you* deem are necessary. You are captain of your ship. Having this information in the forefront of your mind can hold you in good stead as you traverse this thing called life.

Recently I was listening to an American program on radio and the person being interviewed was telling their story about how they spent years tracking down the source of a piece of music that was played when they were put on hold. They loved it and said they would ring at times just to listen to the music. After countless hours of trying to track the source down and after achieving his goal, he discovered that he had not been alone. There were other people who had done exactly the same thing. They had rung just to listen to this music while being placed on hold.

I was enchanted by this story and impressed that he had stuck with his goal for years, not knowing whether he would ever be successful. Given that I work in the leadership development area, this type of behaviour always inspires me. It takes grit and determination and a certain amount of doggedness and can be met with frustration, boredom, and wondering why you are bothering.

In addition to this person being interviewed, another person, who is close to the man, was also interviewed. I was quite shocked and surprised by how nasty he was. Disparaging, horrible rhetoric that put his friend down for having the courage and guts to stay with something for so long, given that he didn't know what the outcome would be.

When the man was interviewed after his 'friend', I noticed a significant change in his demeanour; rather than being excited and proud of his achievements he downplayed what he had achieved and the joy had gone from his voice.

How sad it is. To think he was doing what he wanted, what was important to him, and because of what someone else said he allowed that to dominate. He did not acknowledge himself for the incredible tenacity he had displayed or for staying with his goal.

There is a message in this story for all of us.

Firstly, this scenario is real, and secondly similar scenarios are rolled out far too often and at all stages of our life.

We need to focus on building a strong sense of self so that we can keep pushing forward and not be deterred when others put us down.

We need to believe in ourselves when we don't feel that way.

We need to learn how to fake it until we make it.

We need to be smart with whom we share what we are doing.

We do not need to please people, and we do not need to listen to their negative comments.

We need to be aware that some people do not want us to thrive. They want us to do what they want. They could be jealous of our success. They need to mind their own business and focus on their own life.

We may choose to share information with people who will support and encourage.

We would certainly not share information with dream stealers.

When I am commissioned to design, develop, manage an executive coaching program or leadership development program, I take it seriously. I am only interested in surpassing expected results and put far more into the work and participants than I need to. I am only interested in working with an organisation who is serious about change and who will invest the time and effort into their people to see that the changes deemed necessary are implemented and monitored and then changed again when updating is required.

I see the work I do as an opportunity for the whole organisation – board, executives, managers, employees – to update their systems and processes and their performance in the workplace. They become aware throughout our time together that all changes can be transferred to their personal life and then shared with everyone else they know.

As luck would have it, when I was managing a youth mentoring program, one of the volunteers in the program gave me a good lead in regard to a leadership development program that could be perfect for me.

Still in the process of building an international business, writing and contributing to the media, my time was limited. However, I was not going to pass up this opportunity. The project was cutting edge, had not been trialled before, and connected public, private, and corporate sectors – local, national, and international.

I could only offer a limited number of participants the opportunity to participate in the project and, hence, there were more hands up than I could take on.

After the second session with each participant, it was clear that one participant was only interested in having the leadership program on his CV.

It was my responsibility to assist him to take responsibility for his behaviour and to be very clear that either he did what was required or he would need to leave the program.

After a few sessions, he decided that he would not continue with the program. I had assisted him in a kind, gentle, firm manner to make that decision. He had to explain to his manager why he was not continuing with the program. As a professional this is confronting and challenging but it must be done if I am to be taken seriously

in the industry and to hold myself accountable to my
values and principles.

I doubt whether he considered what occurred as being a
success. I did. He was more likely to think that I was a pain
in the neck. However, in the long term and if he was honest
with himself and thought about it, it could have been a
defining moment in his life.

Success and expecting success are not straight forward.

It will always be from the perspective of the individual.

Our tenacity and doggedness can be confronting for
others and they may feel the need to give us their opinion,
whether we have asked for it or not. Whether we want it
or not.

The more I think about these types of issues and the
deeper I am with the rewrite of this book, I am staggered at
how much time we can spend worrying about what other
people think and not do what is really important to us.

The negative dialogue in our ear can stop us from
moving forward and doing what is really important to us

throughout our whole life if we are not consciously aware of it and stop it. It can drag us down, keep us locked into people-pleasing, and stop us from reaching for the sky and living our incredible, beautiful, fantastic life.

It is your life, do with it what you want, make it count, unravel who you are, dig deep, continue to unravel the you within. When you have a commitment to doing what is ethical and legal, how can you go wrong?

If I had followed other people's agendas, I would not be where I am today.

If I gave up because I had not achieved my goals after one or two tries, I would not be where I am today.

If I let being busy with work life stuff stop me, I would not be where I am today.

If I focused on lack of clarity, I would have given up decades ago and would not be where I am today.

That would have been a great shame because, while the path has been undulating and not always what I wanted or imagined, I would now be missing out on the fantastic, beautiful life I have created for myself.

I love my life and I am so, so glad that I did not let other people's agendas dominate my own and that I did not allow the naysayers to dominate my life.

I have said a few times that it takes courage and determination to live your life the way you want and to be successful.

We need to teach ourselves how to think like a successful person, and then how to act like one.

We need to be aware of what success looks like for us and then go and create it more and more often so that we love it and seek more of it.

We need to learn how to be comfortable with it and stop other people from diminishing who we are.

It is okay to be successful.

It is okay to want it and to focus on having it.

It is normal not to have clarity at times, while at other times, to be crystal clear about what you want and will do next.

That is normal.

That is what being human is.

That is what the human experience is compiled of.

The whiteboard can be similar to your workbook and be a best friend with regular little positive notes reminding you how you want to think and behave. I have found these notes to be life changing, to be nurturing and comforting and they have helped me very much to become successful and to learn to expect success.

One of the personal development workshops I attended in the early years when I was heavily into courses, books, tapes, and workshops and, while incredibly useful and powerful, it was brutal. It threw me around so much emotionally that it took me three months to recover. I felt like I had been put into a bottle of fluid and shaken around for three long months.

What I went through was a difficult time of emotional awakening and, step-by-step, I worked out what I needed to do to achieve the success that was important to me.

Another example of when I had to push through quite a few barriers and do what would bring me the ultimate success I wanted and had worked very hard for was as I sat in the university library, ready to print the final essay for a subject that meant my degree was within arm's reach. With adrenalin running through my veins – with the knowledge that I was so close to being able to have the break I desperately needed, a message came up on the screen asking me if I wanted to do something. I didn't read it. I just pressed the yes button. I waited for the essay to print, but it didn't print. Somehow, I had lost the lot. It could not be found anywhere and the assistants were unable to help me recover it.

I could have given up at that point because I was exhausted but I knew that until the last paper was handed in, I would not have my degree.

Even though this experience occurred years ago it changed who I am and I have never forgotten this. It has held me in good stead since that time and enforced in my mind that any document has to be saved and not only once: a few times if it is important.

I know that when the road blocks and the barriers are broken down, when your life is flowing like a gentle, beautiful stream and you think 'wow, how did that just happen?' and where you can shake your head in wonder, amazement, surprise, and sometimes disbelief because in fact it seems like a dream; you need to claim it.

Own it.

Know that you did it.

The only reason that you are enjoying these wonderful moments in your life is because of all of the hard work you have put into it because you didn't give up when the going got tough.

You did it, and so celebrate.

The successful moment you are experiencing was created by you.

Well done.

When you are experiencing these lovely feelings and
emotions and successes and feeling fantastic, own it, love
it, and savour the moment.

Having experienced these moments many times over
the years, I never tire of them or take them for granted;
I know that it is only because of my hard work that
I am experiencing it yet again. Each time is just as
lovely as the time before and, in addition to savouring
the moment, there is a sense of peace, a feeling of
contentment and gratitude.

On the flip side, when your life is not as you want, ask
yourself 'what is it that I need to do to get back in sync?
How can I have more of what I want?'

I will leave you with some words that came to my mind
when I needed that extra bit of energy and inspiration
to complete the rewrite of this book. I love it when this
happens. These words fill me up when I need them and,
in a convoluted sort of way, gently remind me that my
success with this project and anything else I want to do in

my life is determined by me. Whatever I do begins with one thought and one action and the rest is up to me — *If it's to be: It's up to me.* I hope they inspire you as they did me when you need that extra source of energy and inspiration to complete the task at hand.

*The moral to this story is that when you are just
so sick of the whole thing that you want to burn it
or jump up and down on it, when you feel that you
cannot do any more because you're so exhausted,
when your brain is driving you nuts because you can't
switch it off — you can.*

*If it is something that is important to you —
of course you can.*

*And then when you have completed the goal that you
have worked so hard on and you feel that incredible
feeling of relief and sense of excitement in your gut,
you think to yourself 'yes — it's done.*

*And then when you are jumping up and down for
joy, or dancing around the room and can't wipe the
smile off your face, and you are just so glad that it's
finished, you know — just as important as staying*

with your goal until completion is the need for you –
to take time out and recharge your batteries before
you embark on your next major goal.

Also is the need to acknowledge yourself for having
the courage to stay with the goal and respect
yourself for disciplining yourself through the whole
process, and now to be just as pleased for yourself
as you would be for anyone else who has completed
something very important in their life.

Now you can bask in it and enjoy it and, as one of my
clients said jokingly, 'sip on a daiquiri' when all of the
hard work is done.

WORK LIFE STUFF

ost of us are busy at whatever stage we are in and, from my experience, this does not change. When my kids were little, I was told that it would be easier when the kids went to school. No, it wasn't and hasn't been ever since. There are just other things to do and responsibilities to be kept. If it is not kids, it is something else. That is life.

The part of my life that was the most demanding – and seems to be for everyone else I watch or with whom I have conversed – is when you have kids to raise, plus developing or managing a career, social life, family, community interests, study commitments, and whatever else it is that you have to do.

While I was deliberate with what I chose to work in and study while in the kid stage and ensured I completed what I started, I had not realised at the time that what I was doing was also setting myself up for the next stage of my life and for the rest of my life. Coupled with the other things I have done and continue to do, I have placed myself in an excellent position. I feel incredibly privileged and so, so glad I did it.

Is this what you have done?

How close are you to the next stage of your life?
Have you taken time out to think about how what
you are doing right now will impact the next stage
of your life?

If you have, that's fantastic. If you have not, if it is important to you, you can start right now.

Our life is a continuum, and if we are smart, we will be conscious of that and plan for it. At each juncture, there are emotions to deal with and mental changes that have to be made. Decisions have to be thought about with each action taken. Adjustments need to occur before you can harness the possibilities of the next phase.

For example: when their kids leave home, many think they will dance around and yell 'hooray!' However, when that time does come, it can be a painful period – particularly if you are a maternal person. It can last much longer than you would have thought. You may find that the term 'empty nest syndrome' is not an old wives' tale.

When new generations come along – in advanced economies – many have more available to them than their parents, and it is said that we are much younger than people who were our age (figuratively speaking), than those of earlier generations.

The generation of which I am part of is staying in the workforce longer.

Some want to.

Some need to.

Some people will never retire.

I note also that, in the 21st century, it is the first time in history that there could be two generations of people over 60 in one family. People in their 60s and 70s can still be in the caring role. They may be caring for their children, their parents, or their kids' children. In general, we are living much longer with it said that, in a generation or two, it will be common for people to live until they are 100.

If you cannot wait to retire, beware – very aware of the retirement phase. Whatever age you are – even if this is many years away – take note of this, because you will be at that stage at some time.

Do not just think about the fact that you may be in need of a long break and cannot wait to be able to do this every day. That is not reality. Holidays are one thing where you go away and become refreshed and then go back to a routine. While it is important and valuable to have a holiday, every day being one is yet something else to consider.

There are 24 hours in every day, and 52 weeks x 24 hours to fill each and every year. That is over 8,000 hours, and that's a lot of hours you have to fill each and every year of your life, if you do not have structure and purpose in your life, that challenge you emotionally, physically and mentally.

What might seem like a good idea at the time because of your desire to have a well-earned rest may, in the end, not be the best option for you.

I see people who are intelligent, decent people who have worked hard all of their life, now in their prime, really, because they do have time to spend doing what they want and love. Whether they have got barrels of money or not does not matter as long as they can feed themselves, pay the bills, and live a reasonable life; there are so many things you can do for low cost or for nothing if you take the time to do your research and become creative. The group of people I am talking about either do not know about this or, for whatever reason, do not take advantage of it.

Rather they ride the buses and trains to fill in their day every day and they do that year in and year out. Instead of going to work, they have replaced that with going to the shopping centre. I know one man who used to go to a shopping centre every day – the same one – and talk to the owners and employees of the shops. That was his job. He was more likely to be a pest because business owners have work to do, but that is how he filled his days, weeks, and years.

I see many others wandering around, sitting in the same seat in the shopping centres or in a food court, just watching life and people go by. I see many capable, healthy people sitting in libraries reading the paper and taking out piles of books each week. I make no judgement about this, and if they want to do this then so be it, but they don't look fulfilled or as though they are having much fun. They are just filling in time – hours, days, months, years.

They look bored stiff and lonely and isolated, and they are not tapping into their human potential. They have forgotten all about it.

Not only is this way of living tragic for the participants, it is a tragic waste of human resources. Every aspect of society and community is missing out. These people have a life of experience and, one would hope, much wisdom, which could be put to much better use than is currently being employed. As a society, we lose valuable human resources when everyone is not connected in one way or another. In the end, it can cost community and society significant sums of money.

What happened to their dreams, hopes, and ambitions?

Don't let this happen to yours.

It could easily happen if you do not take charge of your life now – and then at each point in time – and become conscious of the fact that everything we do right now leads onto something else. That consciously or unconsciously, we are indeed planning our life.

The what else we could do is absolutely up to us, and if we do not like the place it is leading to now – whatever age we are – then we need to interrupt that right now, rather than later.

Not doing what I love, not working in an industry that inspires me, challenges me, holds absolutely no interest for me. Why would it? As time marches on, I am better than I was the year before. I know more. I think differently. My priorities are different. I know what I am doing. It has become easy. I know what can be achieved when I am willing to work hard and focus on my goals. I am smarter than I was because I keep challenging myself. My brain feels great when I am giving it a good workout.

My confidence is high because of the same reason. I really look after myself because I know I have to if I want to continue to do what I love, what I'm good at,– what inspires me. I take my needs seriously and respect that I am the same as anyone else and I have to deal with my stuff regularly just the same as anyone else.

Getting old and ageing is not a disease – it is just getting older and ageing, and if you take responsibility for your physical, emotional, and mental requirements, it can be an incredible period of your life.

Age is but a number.
You determine if you become old.
A powerful, important time.

I have noticed that guilt seems to play a big part in the work life stuff area. Most people seem to feel guilty if they spend time developing their own life – they think and feel that they should be doing this or that. They have swallowed the falsehood that in order to be a decent, good person you need to give your life to other people and other causes.

It is a denial of their basic self and fantastic life.

There is a huge difference between being a decent, good person and generous because you want to rather than you think you have to and feel full of guilt if you do not.

When you stop and think about it, why wouldn't you apply the same values and principles to your life as you do and have done for everyone else you've cared for or are caring for now?

So, let's have a look at what you need to pay attention to in regard to your work life stuff.

Think about the questions, answer them, reflect on them, change them, add to them, use them in your personal weekly meeting, and record valuable data that can be used as a benchmark for further and future development.

Questions

- What are the most important things to you right now?
- Have you thought about the next stage of your life?
- What will that be?
- What will it look like?
- What are your goals and dreams then?
- Are you making the most of the stage of life you are in now?
- Can you clearly define what is happening in all areas of your life?
- Are you happy with what you have, or do certain aspects need some tweaking?
- Do you look at the short- and long-term aspect to your work life stuff knowing that it will change as your life changes?

- Do you know the difference between what is urgent, what is very important, what is important, what needs to be done, and what really doesn't need to be done at all?
- How many hours do you work in a week – paid and unpaid?
- How much time off do you have – real time off – not with one eye glued to the work computer at home?
- How much time are you connected to technology?
- Are your devices switched on 24x7?
- How much quality time do you have with yourself?
- How much quality time do you have with those you love?
- What is your diet like?
- How much exercise do you get?
- What do you do to look after your physical, emotional, and mental needs?
- Do you give yourself some time every day to just think, relax and do what you want?
- Do you regularly take holidays?
- How stressed are you?
- How do you determine this?

- How well do you sleep?
- How important is sleep to you?
- Do you just go from day to day, week to week, year to year doing what you think needs doing?
- How often do you complete a personal and professional audit of your life?
- When was the last time you sat down and planned your day, week, month, year?
- Do you want to end up like the retirees I speak of in this chapter?
- If not, how can you set yourself up for success so that you do not end up that way, or that you write another story that has no appeal to you?
- How can you be aware if it is happening and intervene before it becomes an entrenched habit and behaviour?

Life is certainly an interesting phenomenon and it is not until you reach a certain point that you know what that point is like. Hence, the conundrum of those in the workplace and all other areas of society determining what a specific age group should/could/would like to do. Unless the developers are of that origin, how would they know what it will be like when they get to that point? Hence, from my perspective, why so much research and well-meaning policies go pear-shaped and are quite useless for the recipients they have been developed for.

PERSONAL BOUNDARIES

In a work life workshop I developed years ago, one of the topics the participants wanted to discuss – at length – was personal boundaries. All of the women in the room struggled with them, and one said that she thought you just had to accept people the way they were and could not inform them about behaviours you didn't like. I was shocked by this statement and wondered how many other people in the world live their life thinking this way.

We are not responsible for other people's behaviour.

We are responsible for our behaviour.
It is our responsibility to teach others how to treat us.

The bottom line is: if we haven't been clear with someone, then they do not know what we want. If we don't keep telling them until they treat us how we want, then how can they possibly know?

Many people assume that other people should know what they want. This makes no sense. People are not mind readers.

The message needs to be given in the way you would like to receive it. People need to be given time to adjust and we need to be patient with them. It takes time – much time sometimes.

If someone close to me does not have the courage to tell me, I cannot read their mind and I might not be picking up the right signals. And so, rather than having to play a guessing game and taking responsibility for their stuff, it is far better for them to inform me so that I can change and accommodate them if I consider it appropriate and relevant. That can create a much more positive, functional conversation which can bring us closer and we can understand each other better. It can build emotional intelligence and resilience in the relationship when we are respectful, kind, patient, and understanding and get out of our ego.

Personal boundaries run deep.

It is not just what is happening on the surface.

We are conditioned at every stage of our life; it has been drummed into us how to behave, when to do what, and how to do it.

Most of this we don't remember but it's there – it is in our unconscious mind and it dominates and controls us all of our life more than we probably understand or would like to contemplate or accept and acknowledge.

Think back to what it was like when you were little. Can you remember all the times that you were told to do something or not to do something? Do you remember all of the encouragement you received when you had achieved another milestone? Do you remember all of the 'no's' that came your way when you were exploring? Do you remember being told that you had to respect authority? Do you know that it was quite commonplace years ago to be told that if you didn't do something the policeman will come and tell you off or even take you away?

We are taught to fear authority by those who raise us and if not by them, by others in society. It is stored in our unconscious mind and no doubt influences us throughout our whole life.

As parents we use a raft of techniques to control our kids, not because we don't love them or want the best for them, but because raising kids can at times be a hard gig. We use anything that works. Not thinking about the long term impact and consequences on the human being we are raising.

And then when that child grows into an adolescent, think about what they are told to do and not to do and think about the adolescent who is determined to do what they want. They are informed about their inappropriate behaviour often.

The media is full of it as well.

It is full of people who are in authority telling us what to do, what not to do, and the advice keeps pouring out like a never-ending drone. It is constantly presenting us with information and advertising that makes us fearful if we don't do what they are saying.

It is designed that way.

The problem with this is that there is so much different advice that it is enough to make anyone feel confused and ill to boot most of the time. The advertisers and marketers know *exactly* what they are doing. They study our psychological profile and target us specifically and we can be more like a puppet on a string that we would like to think.

So, weave all of this together.

Think long and hard about what you know about the different stages of life and what we are bombarded with at each stage, and then it is no wonder that people have difficulty standing up for themselves and have trouble enacting their personal boundaries.

Add all of the groups in societies to the mix as well and they have their own policies and procedures and the individuals have very clear expectations of how we will behave, what we will do, and what we won't do. And, interestingly, most of the group members follow without questioning. Those who do question are often not viewed favourably, maybe seen as a nuisance or a trouble maker and can become ostracised or leave the group and find another one which is more compatible with their views and beliefs. And that new group will have their policies and procedures and ways of thinking and behaving, but its rules and regulations will be more palatable at that time to the person who has joined.

It is the same with families – there is a code, an unwritten law on how to behave. Each has their own culture and whatever goes on in that family will be by them considered to be normal, whereas someone looking in from the outside would be able to see their flaws. However, if they stay there for long enough, the behaviour will then appear normal to them as well.

It is as though we merge.

We are conditioned from the moment we are conceived into that family culture. It is their way of operating. And we have to conform.

You do not know any different when you are growing up. What you have experienced when you grow up is normal to you. How can you know any different? You do not have the emotional or intellectual skills or the ability to analyse it. You hope that you were born into a functional family and that they have a clue about what they are trying to do with raising their kids.

I note that often people who do not fit in with the family DNA and challenge the behaviours and habits of their upbringing are referred to as the 'black sheep' of the family. I have thought about this for years and wonder about this and, rather than the black sheep, I wonder if they are really the functional ones and everyone else is so stuck in how things must be done that they refuse to change the habits of a lifetime, whereas the black sheep is challenging the status quo.

Personal boundaries are complicated and to understand the background of humans and your family structure is important if you are to unravel and enact your own. Whether you like it or not you will probably continue to seek out people you feel comfortable with and will do so until you decide that you want to change and the other behaviour no longer suits you.

It is one thing to realise that strong personal boundaries are essential to live any sort of quality, decent life where you achieve your goals; where you make yourself a priority; and where you – with kindness and love – advise people how you will be treated and what your absolute bottom line is. It is yet another to be determined to do so and then do it. Sometimes they are easy to implement, while at other times they are challenging.

For me, getting my personal boundaries in order was closely linked to the realisation that I felt too responsible for other people. My first clear insight that I needed to work on this area of my life came to me when I was a young woman. I have worked on them since this time and continue to do so.

A bolt of lightning struck me four years later after I had indeed worked hard and thought that I was further ahead in this area than when I had started.

I was looking to study and knew I'd know what it was when I saw it. This occurred and I never knew at that time just how important this study would be to the overall quality of my life and certainly to my business.

I was studying computer applications. I'd made friends with a woman in the class who was a little younger than me. She was a lovely woman, clearly a decent human being and we had much to talk about and laugh about. Throughout the course it became clear that she did not understand what was being taught. She did not want to ask the teacher for help because she did not want to appear as though she did not understand the material, or for the group to think she was incompetent and stupid.

I love to help people and am only too glad to do so. I didn't find this new knowledge easy but I was keeping up with it and putting extra effort into it at home.

Not having the foresight to know that helping her once would lead to a pattern of behaviour for both of us and cause me angst, I gave her the information she asked for on that day. As the course progressed and she continued to not understand what she was doing I was dogged by her constant requests for assistance.

I did not know how to get out of this situation. I did not want to be rude because I really liked the woman and so, against my better judgement, continued to help her. I would say, if I am honest, that there was a fair amount of fear as well because I didn't want to upset or offend her and didn't know how she would react if I did say no, and how that would impact on us while we were in the same class. Also, when something like this happens, often other memories are triggered, and certainly in this case, my mind jumped back to what it was like in earlier school days. In addition to this, we sat next to each other.

I felt angry, used and it increased my stress levels. It took away the enjoyment of the class. I worried about it during the week, when I was not with her and then when I was there, I just didn't know how to get out of the situation.

I thought long and hard about it and implemented a plan. I decided that moving seats would be appropriate because it would put distance between us. I could then mind my own business, work on my work and she hers. I could do this in the exam as well. I would keep my eyes down and just do what I was there to do. During the exam, I had a feeling that someone was looking at me. I looked up. Yes, it was her and yes, she asked me what to do and yes, I helped her. I just didn't have the heart or emotional fortitude not to.

And guess what?

When the exam results were given out, we were all standing crowded in the corridor next to the entrance to the room while the lecturer told everyone in a loud voice that everyone had passed their exam, except guess who – yes, you guessed right – me. I had failed.

It was a cruel, horrible, brutal moment and I remember how ashamed I felt. It took me a long time to deal with this and it kept coming to my mind year after year and the shame kept coming back along with the other memories.

It was remarkable to see the way this person behaved after receiving the successful mark. She did not thank me for my help and commiserate with me for failing. It was as though she was completely unaware about what had occurred throughout the whole period of study.

Remarkably, I saw her years later and she was still the same: a lovely woman who still had not worked out what she wanted to do with her life.

While I had been working on the 'taking too much responsibility for others habit' for a long time there was clearly much more work to be done and I was not as far along as I thought I was. It was one of those sledge hammer moments you need in order to give you the awareness to make more changes.

Now with years more practise – with learnings under my belt and my radar more finely tuned – I like to think that I would not set myself up for this in the first place and that if by accident it did happen, that I would have the strength and stamina to just get out of it and act dumb towards those requests.

I don't think you ever arrive with personal boundaries. They always have to be worked on and in each stage of our life. Sometimes you will be very good at them and then at other times, you wonder why on earth you didn't stand up to that person and go away feeling angry with thoughts racing through your head as to why you didn't say what you needed and wanted. And spend far too much time thinking about what you would say to them now. I know that when this happens for me, I feel as though there was a wasted opportunity for personal development and I spend far too much time thinking about it and wondering whether I should say something the next time I see them.

Start slowly when you are enacting your personal boundaries and informing others how you want to be treated. Do so only if it is safe. Never put yourself in any danger. Enacting strong personal boundaries is essential if a quality life is to be lived and they need to be monitored. We need to teach people how we want to be treated.

ROAD BLOCKS

This chapter can help you to identify what your road blocks are and then, over time and with much work, you will be able to identify what road blocks you want to change in your life, have clarity about how they impact your life, and why you believe you need to change them.

You can also call road blocks *saboteurs* or *barriers*. They seem to be fairly good mates, and when we are in that space, they seem to have a number of close friends who all hop on board to give us things to work through and challenges to mount.

Road blocks will be different from time to time and throughout different stages of your life. However, all human beings have to contend with similar issues, regardless of how old or young we are; they are just packaged differently.

You may already know some of the things that you do that hinder your progress and success, or you may need to become the observer of your behaviour and life for a while. For example: you may be a person who thinks a lot but doesn't get into action.

You may get caught up in the excitement of a New Year's Resolution but don't follow through with it because the goal you have set is too big and you lose interest. It could be that you don't understand how the body and mind are all connected and that food, exercise, and working with your mind is integral to living your fantastic life.

As you progress with your personal weekly meetings, allow some time to stop and think about your road blocks. Identify which ones you want to work on, and then set up the time and place to do it.

When you have identified what they are, think about the road block and how it looks in your life. The more specific you can be here the better because you will be able to start to know when you are doing it and then stop it.

I find keeping a workbook an essential tool and a sanity saver. Over time, it has become like a best friend and confidante. It gives me insights about myself, and it is like the download facility my computer has, but instead I am downloading information from my brain and this clears my head. I would be lost without it, and if I don't do it regularly I can feel the difference. It helps me to gain the clarity I want and need to be able to live the life I want.

A huge side benefit of using my workbook is that I do not have to talk to or burden other people with my stuff. We all have our own, and it can be incredibly boring to have to listen to people downloading theirs. My workbook enables me to be my own personal-best therapist.

When I started my business, I knew what I wanted to achieve but had no idea how to do it or whether I would be successful. Now, years down the track, I know what I am doing and I am glad I stuck with it. I am a very different person from when I first started. Coupled with the other education and interests I have it has worked well. It was more about unravelling the personal road blocks that has given me the level of success I have attained. I could have educated myself in every area I wanted, but without the inside development and pushing through my road blocks I would not be where I am now.

One of the things that helped me to keep pushing through my road blocks while developing the business – and was something quite unexpected but fantastic – was that, when I'd had enough of it all and felt that I could not keep pushing on with it, I would inevitably listen to someone on the radio, television, read an article, or hear something that would be exactly what I needed to hear at that moment. It would encourage and inspire me and give me the energy to keep moving forward and to complete the task at hand.

One of these people who had a huge influence on me and who would keep popping into my mind was the Kentucky Fried Chicken man. I became aware of what he had gone through to build his business up and that, while the white uniform became his signature presence, he wore it because he had nothing else. He went from door to door – thousands of doors – to sell his wares. He really was my inspiration for a long time.

It can feel like I am trying to break through a thick concrete wall when I am working on a road block. There is generally stress and confusion about it, and I wonder whether what I am doing will eventually lead to peace of mind and my goal.

Often the road block I think I am facing turns out not to be the real issue at all. It is as though there are layers of issues that need to be addressed first that eventually lead to the real road block being dismantled and, after much chipping away, I achieve my goal. It is a wonderful feeling and relief.

I *know* when I have moved through it – it is that freedom feeling in my gut. It feels clean and I know intuitively that another one has gone. And I laugh to myself and say 'yes, I did it – another one gone.' I embrace those moments and enjoy them.

One of the strategies I employ when I am stuck and feel that ball of fear in the pit of my stomach and don't know what to do while being determined to push through is to mentor myself.

I think about what I would do if I felt brave and then do it. I then think about how hard it is – say 2/10 or 8/10 (10 being the highest level). I talk myself through the process and keep practising it until I no longer feel the fear. The time required and level of success varies with this.

In order to prepare for this chapter and to be able to assist you to become aware of whether you would like to make changes in this area of your life, I have thought long and hard about my road blocks and have been honest with myself. I have also spoken to other people and observed human beings in action for a very long time (all ages and levels).

After speaking to other generations and conversing with people from all walks of life about this topic, it seems that there are similarities at whatever age we are. Some people see the benefit of working on their road blocks while others are not the slightest bit interested and do not see any benefit to doing so.

I have thought about what my road blocks are now that I am aware and reminded myself about the many I have worked on and know that, while I would love to tackle all of them, I do not have the time or the inclination to do so.

Some years ago, I also realised that I could spend my whole life focusing only on the past and trying to resolve issues and, fortunately, had a few sledge hammer moments. I realised that I could continue doing this for all of my life and never do it all, and if I did that – guess what – I would not get on with living my life now.

So, there has to be a negotiation with yourself about what you need to work on, how that will impact your life now, and how much you will not work on. This is another one of those contradictions of life that will have to be addressed. They are all over the place. Which ones have you uncovered?

Now, let's get you thinking some more about your road blocks and start to think which (if any) you would like to work on. Remember that you are the driver of your life and do what you want to do and what you are comfortable with. This is your life, live it the way you want and do what will bring you a life you love and where you feel a sense of control over it. (It seems to me that every moment of our life is potentially a '*Sliding Doors*' moment.)

Naturally it's only when you become aware of your road blocks that you can do anything about them. But easy does it: Rome wasn't built in a day and you can't rush these things. I have found that doing this can stir up other emotional issues and I can sometimes not feel very well when I'm doing this.

So, take it easy with yourself and, while I encourage my clients to treat themselves like they do their best friend, I also know that we are not taught how to do this and it can feel weird.

Here are some issues that I and others have become aware of that have caused road blocks. You may choose to think about them and add your own and then include them in your personal weekly meeting.

When you consider the contents of the list and answer the questions, note that there is no shame with this – it just is at this moment in time. We can't change what we don't know and have no hope of moving through road blocks or other stuff if we are not honest with ourselves.

After the list of potential road blocks are some questions for you to think about and also consider in your personal weekly meeting.

Road blocks

- People-pleasing
- Fear, anxiety, stress
- Too busy
- Not willing to commit to the time that change takes
- Believe that other people know far better than you do
- Focus too much on what the media, other people, and advertising tell you what to do
- Don't check your doormat status often enough
- Sit on the fence for weeks, months, years rather than make a decision and get on with it

- Blame the government, current generations, and previous generations for your life now
- Feel responsible for everyone else and look after everyone else's needs and feel put upon
- Feel selfish when you do take the time necessary to work on your own desires, needs, and road blocks
- Allow feeling stuck to stop you from moving forward

Questions

- What does '*road block*' mean to you?
- Which road blocks would you like to work on?
- Which ones can be shelved?
- What are you willing to do to change them?
- How hard are you willing to work?
- How tenacious are you?
- How much time are you willing to commit?
- Are you willing to stay with the process even when it doesn't appear to be moving fast enough and where you do not have the clarity you want and need?
- How will you know when you have broken through a road block?

I wish you well when you are working on your road blocks and, from my perspective, the road blocks are not just about me. Knowing that they are embedded in society at every level in every generation and that many were handed down to me has made it easier for me to let go of or manage the shame I felt and just work on the ones which are relevant to me now.

Life ebbs and flows and I am always learning. The deeper I go within myself, the more I learn about what I want to do and what will bring me the best results for the time invested. I continue to teach myself this and I now enjoy caring for myself and being kind to myself.

I know that it takes courage to even consider looking at my road blocks and I acknowledge myself for that. So, take it easy. Be kind to yourself, and if you feel that you need some help then do so.

There are many fantastic professionals who can help you to develop your personal weekly meeting – a blueprint for your fantastic life. You don't have to go it alone. Always remember that it is just one step at a time that will lead you to where you want to go.

YOUR SUMMATION

We have now come to the conclusion of *If it's to be: It's up to me*, and it is your turn to inform me as to what you have achieved. Learning and understanding this process over a period of 10 weeks, we have covered many topics and you have developed your two small goals. What about your fantastic life? What does it look like now compared to what it looked like when you first began? What successes have you had – even tiny ones? What have you learned about yourself that you didn't know before? Have you dared to allow yourself to dream about what you would love to do and how you would love to live your life? Have you accepted that this is a work in progress for all of your life?

Do you now realise that it is as important to have a systems and processes approach in your personal life as it is in your professional life? Have you thought about what you are willing to compromise on while you are developing and living your fantastic life? How about the areas that you will not compromise on – what are they? What will you have that you don't have now? Who will be in your fantastic life?

Do you know now that it is essential to spend the time researching and thinking about your goal before you jump into action? Was it hard for you to not jump into action, as it is for everyone I know and have worked with? Were you itching to get active before you even knew what you really wanted?

Did you become aware of any habits or behaviours that you want and need to change in order to be able to live your fantastic life? How was that for you? Was it confronting and how did you handle these issues? What new habits and behaviours have you started and why? Have you learned that your workbook can be like a best friend and confidante?

How will you know when you are living a fantastic life?

It is easy to miss when you are living a fantastic life if you don't pay full attention. It is far too easy to get caught up in wanting everything to be perfect before you will be happy. We are bombarded by so much rhetoric and advertising every second of the day that it can stop you from doing anything because of the choices. We are told by many in society that we shouldn't expect to be happy. That we should just get on with it and that our just desserts will come later. We can believe unconsciously or consciously

YOU CAN DO THIS

that it is up to others to make us happy and when they don't, we think it's their fault – that they are to blame.

There is a lot riding on being happy and even knowing what true happiness is. For me, now I know what my fantastic life looks like, and it is rewarding to be able to say this. I know you will be pleased for me when I inform you that the inside story now matches the outside story often enough. I veer off track like anyone else and have built enough memories that my unconscious mind tries to bring me back gently to square one. It does this with an insight or relevant thought, and through this process I can become aware that indeed I have gone off on a bit of a detour. At these times I have those chance conversations or look at something or hear someone talking that triggers what I need to know. Other times the reminders need to be more like a sledge hammer moment before I get it again.

It does not mean that everything in my life is perfect or as I want, but it means that I feel well, emotionally, mentally, and physically enough of the time, and that I am achieving and doing enough of what is important to me enough of the time, and that I am very focused on now, next week, next year, and my long-term goals. It also means that I do experience the magic of life often enough for me. It means that I don't take anything for granted and I have no interest in being labelled or adhering to them.

Given I work in the area of leadership development and my love of learning, you will not be surprised to know that I continue to educate myself in many areas and then refine that knowledge and link it to what I do. That's just what I do. That's what I love. And because of my interest in many areas, I like to look at the gaps in society.

It is not commonplace to teach people how to be emotionally successful.

That is a gap.

We are not taught how to plan our life or develop a blueprint.

That is a gap.

We are told by some that we should just get on with it and bypass the pain that we are feeling and that is a *huge* gap. We dismiss and minimise what humans have to deal with throughout their life far too much.

That is a gap.

This approach does not set us up for success or teach us how to live a fantastic life, rather we tell people by how we behave and by what we say – 'have a cuppa', 'that'll do it.'

Certainly, I do not know all of the answers, but I have many ideas and I know that what I am talking about and what I have discussed works with every age group and generation just as well as it does with senior executives when people are willing to work hard to achieve their desired outcomes. And what I do know is that we would be wise to take stock of what we are doing with the current generation: stop using old methodologies that do not work, work out how we can make changes that will give us the results we want and need for the members of society to thrive and to be able to manage their life and be able to get on with it.

We need to stop talking about what's wrong and get into action and. of course, take the time to measure every single thing we do and refine our strategies as we need to, to ensure that those strategies work well.

One-size hat does not fit all and that is why what I do seems to be so effective.

The model is changed to suit the age and requirements of each person and group I work with.

Anyone I have ever known struggles with their life at times – no one is immune from this – and for the many people who really struggle with their life, how wonderful would it be to be able to teach them how to move through their issues? Think about the ones who are addicted to whatever it is they are addicted to and need licit and illicit drugs to get through their day.

Wouldn't it be fantastic to assist the millions of others who would like to improve the quality of their life just with the day-to-day issues that they face?

Throughout my life and career, I have been part of a range of collectives that focus on what I discuss in this book. It is always a privilege to be able to assist people to work out a way forward that impacts the current generation, knowing that it will impact future generations.

If you have a look, deep inside society, it will not take you long to realise that what we are doing in this area is not working anywhere near as well as it could. There are far too many people who tragically fall by the wayside and slip through the cracks of school and society. There are far too many highly intelligent people who never unravel this or even know they are intelligent.

Tragically also is the fact of people taking prescription drugs because they think and believe they will make them happy is increasing annually. It is said that people now feel much more comfortable asking for them, whereas they used to feel ashamed. Now, instead of slinking into the medico's office, many go with their shopping list, requesting a range of licit drugs they want prescribed. Sadly, they don't look at, don't care enough about, or are not told about the side effects, whereas with illicit drugs we are told often what the side effects are and that we should avoid them at all costs.

I know people (and have known for years) who take this medication and from what I see, while they do take the pressure off what is happening right now, they are not magic pills and the recipients still need to work on their stuff if they want to live their fantastic life. Rather than seeing this way of living as a long-term solution, we could teach people how to manage the issues that they need to address in their life. We could help them manoeuvre the difficult bits and help them to learn how to build resilience so that they can come through the difficult periods a much stronger, more resilient human being.

To interrupt this cycle, we need to give people a foundation that they can build upon which creates generational change. By doing so, we change the world incrementally, bit by bit, person by person, family by family, group by group until it becomes entrenched in people's minds with habits and behaviours and then is passed down through the line and to other generations. We could continue to do this until a tipping point occurs and then it becomes the natural thing to do; it becomes just normal for us to develop ourselves and others with the life skills and abilities to develop their own blueprint for their life and teach them that they can indeed live a fantastic life.

Ideally, we would start very early and get people used to the idea that they do have the inner resources to work their stuff out and that, along with guidance, support, encouragement, they will do far more than this. They will unpack who they really are and maximise their DNA and the culture in which they live. And, along with this, learn early that there is no such thing as 'one potential'; they can learn that their potential is unlimited when it is coupled with tenacity, hard work, and all of the other things I speak of in *If it's to be: It's up to me*, and then, as I say often: once they have worked it out, they can share that wonderful knowledge with every single person they know and love. They will be a beacon of light even when they are not conscious of being one.

It has been a pleasure to work with you and to rewrite *If it's to be: It's up to me*. It is now much more comprehensive than it was when first published. I sincerely hope that the book will assist you to put your life into perspective, whatever your professional level or stage of life, and to continue to *think* about everything you do and to examine why you do it and what you really want in your life. It is only when you continue to microscopically examine your life that you can unravel it and implement best practice for you and for those you love.